7 Stages of Teeth presents

Chopper Optional

Recipes for
the recently toothless

Copyright © 2016 Donna Wylie
All rights reserved.
Book and cover design by Rick Wylie
ISBN: 10-1535055901
ISBN: 13-978-1535055901

Table of Contents

1. Introduction
3. Liquids
4. Smoothies & Smooshies
5. Chocolate Protein Powder Drinks
7. Vanilla Protein Powder Drinks
9. Breakfast Anytime
11. Hindsight Hints
12. Main Meals
22. Desserts
24. Food Hacks
26. Helpful Links

To Rick for his tireless dedication to my mental and physical well-being.

Introduction

A Brief History of the Year I Got Teeth for My Birthday

This book was born from necessity. In 2015, on my 61st birthday, I had 21 teeth pulled and immediate dentures placed in my numb, bloodied and abused mouth. I was in no shape to chew!

The post extraction instructions from the dentist advised a diet of liquids and soft foods while my mouth healed. The sheet suggested foods like broth and yogurt. That's all well and good if you are talking about a matter of days, but I was looking at a matter of weeks!

I was fortunate to have the help of my husband Rick as my "denture co-pilot". He completed endless circuits of the grocery store, searching out food that I could eat without having to chew. He experimented with ways to cook and prepare regular food so it could be consumed without much effort on my part. He "sympathy ate", sharing my mushy meals.

Together, we created this compilation of "Chopper Optional" meals for the recently toothless and their copilots. I hope you find nourishment here for your soul as well as your body. To paraphrase a popular quote, "keep calm and chew on!"

Donna Wylie; Mesa AZ; 2016

Donna Wylie

Liquids

Be sure to keep well hydrated, and nourished. This is where your denture co-pilot can be invaluable. My first day or two after the procedure was spent recuperating from the physical and mental trauma I had endured. I had no ambition or desire to cook or eat. Rick made sure I was well rested and well fed so my body could get on with the business of healing.

Straws -The problem with online searches is the amount of conflicting information. Some sites advised against using straws after dental work, because it would dislodge clots and slow healing. Other sites disagreed, saying the suction from a straw wasn't sufficient to do any damage. You should always check with your dentist to get the best advice for your particular situation.

Here are some suggestions for liquids:

Chicken or Beef broth - My favorite brand is "Better Than Bouillon", a flavorful, healthier alternative.

Vegetable juice - Add a sprinkling of ground cayenne or turmeric, or a dash of hot sauce. All help relieve pain.

Chocolate milk - Pre-made or mix your own, using your favorite syrup. Add a dash of ground nutmeg or cinnamon - natural pain-killers - or mix in espresso powder or brewed coffee for your own coffee shop drink.

Cola Milk - Just what it sounds like - your favorite cola, mixed half and half with your favorite milk. My favorite treat!

Liquid yogurt or kefir - Ready to drink, easy nutrition. Stock up for those first days!

Instant breakfast shakes/Milkshakes

Smoothies (see separate section for recipes)

Fruit juice

Note: for a soothing first-day treat, try freezing any of these recipes or your favorite beverage in mini cubes. If you can't find small cube trays, use regular size and crush them in your blender or food processor. The cubes or ice chips are flavorful, and help soothe sore gums.

Smoothies and Smooshies
Made with Whey Protein Powder

A word about protein powder: I was skeptical about trying protein powder but my sister raved about the taste, and provided me with numerous recipes for smoothies that she likes. In the weeks following my dental procedure, when I was unable to chew, this powder helped ensure that I got the protein and nutrients my body needed to heal. The powder comes in various flavors, including chocolate, vanilla, coffee and strawberry. You owe it to yourself and your health to try it!

Chocolate Protein Powder Drinks

For each of these recipes, the instructions are simple – put the ingredients in a blender, mix, and enjoy!

Chocolate Peanut-Butterscotch Smoothie

1 cup milk (any kind)

½ - ¾ cup cold water

1 cup ice cubes

1 scoop chocolate protein powder

1 large Tablespoon peanut butter

1 Tablespoon butterscotch instant pudding, dry mix

Cocoa-Hazelnut Latte

1 ½ cups milk

10 ice cubes

2 scoops chocolate protein powder

2 Tablespoons vanilla yogurt

2 Tablespoons prepared hazelnut coffee

Chocolate-Strawberry Smoothie

1 - 2 scoops chocolate protein powder
1 cup cold water
4 – 6 ice cubes
8 whole, frozen strawberries

Chocolate-Peppermint Smoothie

1 – 2 scoops chocolate protein powder
1 teaspoon peppermint extract
3 – 4 ice cubes
1 cup cold water

Chocolate-Covered Peanut Butter Banana Smoothie

1 - 2 scoops chocolate protein powder
1 cup milk
1 medium, frozen, sliced banana
2 Tablespoons peanut butter

Power Shake

1 – 2 scoops chocolate protein powder
½ cup prepared coffee, cooled
½ cup milk
2 teaspoons cocoa mix

Choco-Coconut Shake

1 scoop chocolate protein powder
1 cup coconut milk
2 ½ teaspoons chocolate instant pudding, dry mix
1 Tablespoon coconut extract

Coffee to Go
1 – 2 scoops chocolate protein powder
1 ½ cups milk
1 scoop coffee-flavored ice cream

Chocolate-Covered Blueberry Power Shake
1 scoop chocolate protein powder
1 packet chocolate breakfast drink powder
1 ½ cups milk
1 cup frozen blueberries
6 – 8 ice cubes

Vanilla Protein Powder Drinks

Vanilla Coffee Latte
2 scoops vanilla protein powder
½ cup coffee yogurt
1 ½ cups milk

Almond Cherry-Vanilla Shake
1 scoop vanilla protein powder
1 cup vanilla almond milk
½ cup frozen, pitted cherries
6 ice cubes

Strawberry-Banana Smoothie

1 scoop vanilla protein powder
3 – 4 whole, frozen strawberries
½ banana, sliced and frozen
1 cup cold water
5 – 6 ice cubes

Apple Pie Shake

1 - 2 scoops vanilla protein powder
1 cup milk
½ cup vanilla yogurt
½ cup applesauce
Pinch of cinnamon
Pinch of nutmeg

Peanut-Butter Jelly Shake

1 - 2 scoops vanilla protein powder
1 cup milk
1 Tablespoon smooth peanut butter
1 teaspoon strawberry jam

Berry-Orange-Vanilla Shake

2 scoops vanilla protein powder
2 cups orange juice
1 teaspoon vanilla extract
2 – 3 whole, frozen strawberries
½ banana, sliced and frozen
4 – 5 ice cubes

Coffee Almond Latte

1 - 2 scoops vanilla protein powder

1 cup cold water

½ cup coffee yogurt

1 teaspoon vanilla or almond extract

Nut Lovers Smoothie

1 - 2 scoops vanilla protein powder

1 cup almond milk

1 Tablespoon smooth almond butter

2 Tablespoons smooth peanut butter

6 – 8 ice cubes

Orange Cream Dream Shake

1 - 2 scoops vanilla protein powder

1 ½ cups orange juice

3 – 4 ice cubes

Breakfast Anytime

Instant Hot Cereal - Dress up a packet of your favorite hot cereal by mixing in applesauce or pureed fruit. Baby food works well, and has the added benefit of additional vitamins and minerals.

Graham Crackers and Milk - A favorite from my childhood! Simply break up crackers, add milk and stir. The crackers turn soft and easy to eat.

Coffee and Donuts – Start with a cup of your favorite coffee, hot or cold. Crumble in some powdered donuts (cinnamon sugar works as well) and stir until the donuts are thoroughly soaked in coffee, and soft enough to eat.

No-Fuss, Overnight Oatmeal
Per Serving:
½ cup oatmeal, 1 minute quick-cook type (Not instant)
¼ cup of your favorite flavor yogurt
¼ – ½ cup milk (any kind)
1 – 3 Tablespoons brown sugar
Sprinkle of ground cinnamon and ground ginger

Mix well, cover, and refrigerate overnight. Eat cold, like a delicious, nutritious pudding!

Substitutions:
Coffee flavored yogurt and chocolate milk
Strawberry flavored yogurt, almond milk; mix in 1 Tablespoon strawberry jam
Peach flavored yogurt, vanilla almond milk, 1 Tablespoon peach jam

The combinations are endless! Use your imagination and your favorite flavors!

Chocolate – Peppermint Oatmeal for Two

2 scoops chocolate protein powder
1 cup vanilla ice cream
1 cup oatmeal, 1 minute quick-cook type (Not instant)
2 cups milk
½ cup water
½ teaspoon peppermint extract

You can do this as an overnight oatmeal, or blend and enjoy as a breakfast smoothie!

Eggs – Scrambled or soft-boiled are easiest to eat, with minimal chewing needed. Add in some ricotta, Parmesan or sharp cheese for extra protein. You can also grind up mushrooms and ham in your food processor. Add a dash of hot sauce or taco sauce for spice.

Hindsight Hints

Invest in a food processor and blender. You can use one appliance if it can blend as well as grind. Eating is all about the flavor. Ground ham tastes just as good in an omelet and is easier to eat when you have a sore mouth.
Pace yourself! In the beginning, when I first started eating solid foods again, I could only eat one "chewy" meal per day, then it was back to "mushie" meals the rest of the day. Even small efforts at chewing were exhausting at first, and extremely time-consuming.

Main Meals

Macaroni & Cheese – Use your favorite boxed brand, prepared according to package directions. Mash with a potato masher, or process briefly, adding more milk as needed.

Tuna Salad – Mash up or process the tuna, to break it up well. Add in extra mayo to desired consistency; mix in 1/8 – 1/4 teaspoon celery salt. Can garnish with soft bread crumbs – just take a slice of bread and process to crumb texture. Provides all the flavor of a tuna sandwich without the work.

Mushroom Soup and Bread – Another favorite from my childhood. Mix 1 can cream of mushroom soup with 1/2 – 3/4 can of water. Mix & stir, heat over medium heat until desired temperature.
Butter 2 slices of soft, white or wheat bread. Trim off crusts and cut bread in 1" chunks. Dip or soak bread in soup until soft.

Mashed Potatoes And... – Stock up on instant mashed potatoes. They cook up quickly, are easy to eat, and can be prepared a number of ways. To name a few –

Mashed potatoes and gravy – use canned gravy for a no-fuss, satisfying meal.

Mashed potatoes and turkey - grind some leftover, cooked turkey or chicken. Add it to a jar of turkey or chicken gravy. Tastes like thanksgiving!

Mashed potatoes and cheese sauce - your favorite cheese sauce, mild or spicy and sour cream. For a Mexican style, add some taco sauce.

Mashed potatoes and chili - grind canned or homemade chili in the food processor.

Note: All of these toppings work great over rice as well.

Naked Bean and Cheese Burrito - Heat a cup of refried beans and place on a plate. Top with nacho cheese sauce, taco sauce, guacamole and sour cream. You can also add a sprinkling of ground tortilla chips (just toss a handful of chips in your food processor and pulse for a few seconds).

Ham Salad - As long as you're grinding ham, set aside some for ham salad. Mix the ham with plenty of mayo; add a dash of juice from a jar of sweet pickles, and a sprinkle of celery salt. Top with soft bread crumbs.

Make Mine an Enchilada – Mix together refried beans, cheese and taco sauce. Place a heaping spoonful on a corn tortilla and roll up (do Not use flour tortillas). Place filled tortillas, seam side down in a lightly greased baking dish. Cover with your favorite enchilada sauce. Bake, uncovered, at 350 for about 20 – 25 minutes. Serve with guacamole and sour cream.

The corn tortillas will cook to a fork-tender consistency that breaks apart easily. You can also add meat such as chicken, pork or beef. Just grind the meat finely before adding. The food processor can handle that task in seconds!

Bean/Split Pea Soup – For additional flavor and protein, add ground ham. You can also add ground, cooked carrots.

Chicken Salad – Grind some cooked chicken breast; add a sprinkle of poultry seasoning. Top with soft bread crumbs.

Canned Pasta – My favorite are pasta rings in tomato sauce. I add pepper and some ketchup, to "perk up" the flavor. If you want the kind with franks or meatballs, just be sure to cut up or process the meat to a comfortable size.

Game Dogs – Grind beef franks. Sauté lightly in olive oil. Mix in ketchup, mustard, and onion powder. Top with soft bread crumbs. Enjoy while cheering for your favorite team!

Fish – You'll want to choose a kind that flakes easily, like cod, tilapia, or catfish. Frozen fish sticks work fine, just mash them up a bit after cooking.

Add extra nutrition to your meals with mashed vegetables, such as:
Canned green/wax beans – cooked and mashed
Steamed carrots – cooked and mashed
Steamed cauliflower – cooked and mashed

Chili Dogs – Grind beef franks and canned chili. Heat; top with soft bread crumbs.
Got a favorite hotdog topping? Grind the ingredients and get eating! Remember, it's all about the taste!

Seafood Scampi – Start with your favorite seafood, cooked – shrimp, crab, lobster, scallops, or any combination. Grind, mix with garlic butter and sauté until hot. Goes great with unstuffed mushrooms.

Unstuffed Mushrooms – Grind fresh mushrooms; sauté in garlic butter. Stir in ricotta cheese and soft bread crumbs. Serve!

Seafood Alfredo – add ground seafood to a jar of Alfredo sauce and heat. Serve over hot, cooked pasta. I found spaghetti was easier for me to handle with my new teeth. I simply cut it into bite-sized pieces. Experiment to see what size and shape of pasta is easiest for you.

Biscuits and Gravy
Cooked chicken (leftover, or from a rotisserie chicken from the deli), ground
One jar of chicken gravy
Prepared biscuits
Add ground chicken to gravy and heat. To serve, let biscuits soak in gravy until softened, or crumble biscuits over gravy and chicken mixture. Serve with steamed, well-done baby carrots.

Scalloped (Mashed) Potatoes
Substitute mashed potatoes and ground ham in your favorite scalloped potatoes recipe.

Spaghetti and Meatballs
1-pound ground turkey
1 jar spaghetti sauce (Non-chunky)
1 cup small pasta (like ditalini or spaghetti, broken in 1" pieces)
In a deep frypan, over medium heat, brown the ground turkey, being sure to break the meat up well. Add the sauce, dry pasta and ½ - 1 cup hot water. Simmer, stirring occasionally, until the pasta is well done. Serve with grated Parmesan cheese and hot pepper flakes.

Mashed Potato Salad
To cold, mashed potatoes, add:
Ground, hard-boiled egg; Mayo; Dash of pickle juice (sweet or dill); Paprika, celery salt, and salt & pepper to taste

Chicken Enchiladas

1 – 2 cups cooked, ground meat
1 – 2 cups shredded cheese (I like sharp cheddar but you can use mild cheddar or a combination of the two)
1 – 2 Tablespoons sour cream
½ – ¾ cup enchilada sauce (from large can)
6 – 12 corn tortillas (do not use flour tortillas; corn softens and will be easier to eat)

Mix together meat, cheese, sour cream and enchilada sauce. Spread ½ cup enchilada sauce in 8" x 11" casserole dish.

Put heaping Tablespoon of meat mixture on tortilla, roll up, place seam side down in dish. Continue filling tortillas until all meat mixture is used. Cover tortillas with remaining enchilada sauce and sprinkle with more cheese.

Cover dish with foil; bake at 350 degrees for 35 min. serve with additional sour cream.

Chickeny Carrot Soup

2 ½ cups sliced carrots (about 5 medium) OR
1 – 10 ounce package frozen sliced carrots
4 – 6 cups chicken broth, divided
1 ½ teaspoon curry powder (or to taste)
1 teaspoon lemon juice

Simmer carrots in 2 cups chicken broth in covered saucepan, over medium heat, 18 – 20 minutes or until tender. Cool. Process in blender until smooth. Return to saucepan.

Stir in curry powder and remaining 2 – 4 cups chicken broth.

Bring to a boil over medium heat, stirring constantly. Reduce heat; simmer, uncovered, for 10 minutes to develop flavor. Mix in lemon juice, stir, and serve.

4 – 6 servings, 1 cup each.

This soup freezes well; make ahead.

Taco Night –

1-pound ground chicken or turkey
1 packet taco seasoning
15-ounce can refried beans

In a saucepan over medium heat, cook meat until browned, being sure to break the meat up well. Mix in taco seasoning according to package directions, stirring well to combine. Add in refried beans and continue cooking until mixture is thoroughly heated.

Serve with taco sauce, cheese sauce, and sour cream. Sprinkle with crushed nacho cheese flavored chips. 4 servings.

Pizza Pockets

1 - 8-ounce tube refrigerated crescent rolls
¼ cup pizza sauce
½ cup finely shredded mozzarella cheese
4 - ounces pepperoni, ground
4 - ounces mushrooms, ground
1 egg, beaten
¼ teaspoon garlic powder
½ teaspoon Parmesan cheese

* Preheat oven to 375 degrees. Lightly grease cookie sheet.
* Unroll dough and separate into 2 rectangles; seal perforations.
* Spread 2 Tablespoons pizza sauce on half of one rectangle, to within 1 inch of edge.
* Sprinkle 4 Tablespoons of cheese over sauce; add half of the pepperoni and mushrooms.
* Carefully fold other half of the rectangle over the filling. Seal edges with a fork. Repeat process for other rectangle of dough.
* Prick each rectangle with a fork several times, to allow steam to escape.
* Brush top of each pocket with egg, sprinkle with garlic powder and Parmesan.
* Bake 15 – 20 minutes, until deep golden brown.

Cottage Cheese Delight

Author's Note: I thought about calling this "I-Can't-Believe-I-Love-This-Salad!", because I am *not* a fan of cottage cheese. But in the days following my procedure it became my favorite food to the point of obsession! Perhaps it was the yummy taste combination. Perhaps it was the easy texture. Perhaps it's because it tastes like dessert. Whatever the reason, it was an easy, delightful way of getting protein, calcium, B vitamins and Vitamin A in my diet. Try it on your cottage cheese hater!

1 – 16-ounce container small curd cottage cheese
1 – 3-ounce box of your favorite flavor of gelatin
1 – 8-ounce container frozen whipped topping
1 – 15-ounce can mandarin oranges, drained well
Mix dry gelatin into cottage cheese until well blended. Blend in frozen whipped topping. Fold in oranges. Chill at least 3 hours before serving (IF you can wait this long!)

Desserts
Because, ya Gotta have dessert!

Peaches n' Cream
Can use fresh, frozen, or canned peaches. Grind in your food processor, warm briefly in a microwave-safe serving dish.
Top with a dash of cinnamon, and whipped cream or a scoop of vanilla ice cream.

Apple Almost-Pie
1 cup applesauce
½ cup graham cracker crumbs
¼ teaspoon apple pie spice
Put applesauce in a microwave-safe serving dish; warm briefly. Top with apple pie spice (can sub cinnamon and nutmeg), graham cracker crumbs, and whipped cream.
If you don't have graham cracker crumbs, you can substitute cookie crumbs. Or use wheat germ for a nutty flavor and added nutrients.

Root Beer Float
In a tall glass, put 2 scoops vanilla ice cream. Fill glass with root beer. Enjoy!
If you prefer, you can place ingredients in blender and process briefly, until smooth but still thick.

Chopper Optional

Gelatin Salad
You don't have to eat plain gelatin! Just use your food processor to grind your favorite mix-ins. Ex: carrots, apples, pecans, canned or fresh fruit, etc!

Milk and Cookies
For all you cookie dunkers out there!
8-ounces milk
Your favorite wafer cookies (chocolate, vanilla, ginger snap, lemon, Etc!)
Break cookies into chunks, put in milk until soft.

Ice Cream Sandwiches
These rapidly became my favorite dessert after my procedure. They are easy (just requires a walk to the freezer or a helpful spouse); and they have my two favorite treats – cookies and ice cream. Plus, they are soft enough to eat with or without teeth.
What's not to like?!

Pumpkin Smooshie Pie
1 container chocolate or vanilla yogurt
1 – 2 Tablespoons canned pumpkin puree
¼ - ½ teaspoon pumpkin pie spice
Mix together, top with 1 – 2 Tablespoons graham cracker crumbs

Chia Pudding

¼ cup chia seeds

1 cup vanilla almond milk

2 – 3 teaspoons honey

¼ - ½ teaspoon cinnamon

Mix, refrigerate overnight or at least 8 hours.

Food Hacks:

Corn on the Cob - By all means, roast it, steam it, leave it raw, whatever your pleasure. Once the corn is prepared, it can be cut off the cob. Same great taste, easier to eat. Depending on your "tooth-abilities", you can eat it as is, or grind the kernels in your food processor along with butter, S & P and a little milk.

Don't let fear and/or peer pressure make you avoid barbecues. My father-in-law has dentures and loves to include corn on the cob, which he calls the ultimate challenge for people with dentures. He really wants me to join him in his "cob conquering." But as I tell him, I never liked to eat corn on the cob, always preferring to cut it off. That way, the butter stays where I like it (on the corn), and my hands and face don't get greasy. I get the same great taste, just in a neater package!

Chopper Optional

Peanut butter – This childhood staple (and adult comfort food) used to scare me. After all, it's – sticky! Pair it with white bread and you have the ultimate stick-to-the-roof-of-your-mouth nightmare.
I'm not a peanut butter addict, but I do enjoy a good PB&J sandwich every now and again.

The trick to peanut butter is make sure it's covered on both sides. This can be done with just bread, or bread and jam. It's much easier to manage if you aren't biting directly into the sticky goodness. Once you get a bite in your mouth, you can quickly maneuver it to your back teeth to chew.

Another trick is to either heat it or freeze it. Toasting the bread will make the peanut butter soft, and runny. Freezing it will give it a consistency not unlike a peanut butter cup.

Helpful Links

www.MedicineNet.com

www.FamilyHealthOnline.ca

www.StratfordDentureClinic.com/faq.html - This site, by a denture clinic, has a wealth of information!

www.DentalAssociates.com – Another site by a dental clinic, it has comprehensive information on dental implants.

www.MyDentureCare.com/en-us - A bit of a commercial, but there is some great advice.

www.DentureLiving.com/en-us - Another product advertisement, but with some excellent advice as well. This site also has an online community.

http://thedenturepeople.co.uk/your-new-dentures/ - UK site, with lots of information. This link tells what to expect with dentures.

http://www.nhs.uk/conditions/dentures/Pages/Introduction.aspx - Another UK site, great general information.

Chopper Optional

http://dentalcarematters.com/how-to-clean-dentures/ - Comprehensive cleaning advice from a dentist.

https://www.dentistry.utoronto.ca/dpes/prosthetic/patients/denture-soft-liner-patient-version - Information on soft relines. Also good source of general information.

http://www.dentalfearcentral.org/fears/gagging/ - Taming the gag reflex, along with a wealth of other information.

http://lethow.com/health/stop-gag-reflex/ - More information on controlling the gag reflex.

Notes:

Notes:

Made in the USA
Columbia, SC
02 June 2025